the day i was

BAPTIZED

PAM LUCAS

HAL HARRISON

the day i was

BAPTIZED

United Church Press

Cleveland, Ohio

United Church Press, Cleveland, Ohio 44115

© 1998 by Pam Lucas and Hal Harrison

Printed in China on acid-free paper

03   5 4 3 2

ISBN 0-8298-1279-2

the day i was

BAPTIZED

THIS BOOK IS PRESENTED TO

(name of child)

ON THE DAY OF YOUR BAPTISM
BY

(name of church)

ON

(date)

(minister)

(representative of the congregation)

To the Minister and the Church:

This book is designed to assist parent(s)/guardian(s) in telling their child about Baptism and what it means, to help the child understand the importance of the promises made on that occasion, and to encourage the child to see the relationship between Baptism and Confirmation. We hope this will be a book that a child will cherish and will love to look through—like a family photo album.

You can help tell this story by:

- Filling in the words of your church's baptismal formula on page 8.
- Inserting photos of the exterior and interior of your church, your minister, and the baptismal font.
- Keeping copies of the day's bulletin, your church's baptismal promises, and other important documents.
- Providing a way for additional photos of the child, the child's family, and the congregation to be taken on the day of Baptism.
- Writing a letter telling of the church's hopes for the one baptized on page 11.
- Encouraging and helping the parent(s)/guardian(s) to write their own words of hope on page 12.

The minister may want to use this book as a tool for sharing the sacredness of the promises and the meaning of Baptism with the parent(s)/guardian(s) as they plan for the service.

To the Parent(s)/Guardian(s):

Your child will ask many times while growing up: "How? When? Where? What? Why?" But when your child asks, "Was I baptized?" what will you say?

This book will help you answer:

h o w   w h e n   w h e r e   w h a t   w h y

You can help tell the story by sharing this book with your child as he or she grows in knowledge and understanding of the Christian life and faith.

You can help by filling in the appropriate information and reading it to and with your child over the years.

You can help fulfill the promises you made on the day of your child's Baptism by helping your child grow up to confirm the faith you professed on his or her behalf at Baptism. Confirmation is the time when a young person baptized early in life has an opportunity to make public a personal profession of faith.

You can help make this connection between the faith you brought to the child's Baptism and the faith you hope your child will confirm by:

- Taking time right now to write a letter to your child which shares your hopes for your child's life of faith on page 12.
- Bringing your child to church school.
- Worshiping with your child.
- Modeling a life of faithful discipleship.

"Go therefore and make disciples of all nations,

baptizing them in the name of the Father and of the Son

and of the Holy Spirit."

—MATTHEW 28:19

baptized

On the day I was baptized, _____ *(date)* _____,

I was brought to _____ *(name of church)* _____.

[insert picture of church exterior]

It was in _____ (name of town) _____.

The weather was _____.

And I was _____ (years/months/days) _____ old.

[insert picture of child]

ME

Some other people who loved me came with me:_____

_____

_____

_____

_____

relatives
        friends

There were many other people in church that day.

The church is a place where people come to worship God.

$$\left[\text{insert picture of church interior}\right]$$

In church, people say: "Thank you, God,

for life, for the world, for people to love, and for children like me!"

We said some prayers and sang some songs and listened to the words of God from the Bible. When it was time for me to be baptized, I was brought to this place.

The name of the minister who baptized me was _____.

$$\left[\text{insert picture of minister}\right]$$

The minister talked about Jesus loving the little children. The minister talked to all the people about loving little children. The minister asked my parent(s)/guardian(s) and godparent(s) to make some promises about loving me and helping me grow up to love Jesus. They promised to show me what it means to love Jesus every day in every way. They promised to bring me to church to worship God and to learn about Jesus.

[insert picture of parent(s)/guardian(s)/godparent(s)]

Then the minister asked all the people to promise to help me grow up to be Jesus' disciple. The minister talked about the water of Baptism. Water helps things grow and helps keep things clean. Water was important in the Bible. The minister said a prayer about the water. The minister used water to baptize me!

And what did I do? I _____

_____ (cried, slept, looked around, etc.) _____

The water of Baptism helps me to grow up to love Jesus and will help me live like a disciple of Jesus. Disciples of Jesus help other people no matter what they need, and love other people no matter who they are.

These are the words the minister said when I was baptized: _____

_____

_____

_____

The minister prayed for me and asked God to help me grow up and to help my parent(s)/guardian(s) and godparent(s) love and care for me and keep the promises made today.

[insert picture of child with parent(s)/guardian(s)/godparent(s)]

On the day I was baptized, I was named as a beloved child of God. I was claimed as a member of the family of God. Now I'm not just part of my own family. I'm part of a much bigger family called the church.

$$\Big[\text{insert picture of members of the congregation}\Big]$$

We worship together and learn about God together. We do God's work together and we have fun together. And when I get older, I will have a chance to tell everyone in the church that I, too, love Jesus. I will tell everyone that I want to live my life as a disciple of Jesus. That day is called Confirmation!

The church's hopes and prayers for me on my day of Baptism:

_____

_____

_____

_____

_____

_____

_____

_____

_____

My family's hopes and prayers for me on my day of Baptism:

_____

_____

_____

_____

_____

hopes

_____

_____

_____

_____

Now when someone asks me, "What is Baptism?" I can say, "Let me tell you my story."

And I can share with them this book.